THE FIRST TO GET THIS FAR

A Memoir of Resilience, Rhythm and Renewal

by

Wanda Rogers

THE FIRST TO GET THIS FAR

Published by Wanda Rogers

ISBN: 979-8-9930786-1-8

First Edition: January 2026

Printed in the United States of America

10 9 8 7 6 5 4 3 2 1

This Is For:

My mother,

who turned motion into shelter and made every change feel survivable.

I learned how to keep going by watching you create warmth wherever we arrived.

For Sean, represented by Brandon,

who came into my life and stayed. You were a steady place in a shifting world and a quiet yes when everything else hesitated.

You showed me that some forms of love do not hurry—they hold.

And for the moments that slowed me without stopping me,

for the roads that curved instead of closing,

and for the gentle guidance that never needed a name.

This is for the version of me who kept walking, who trusted the bend, and who learned that arrival can be quiet.

This dedication is for the journey that took its time and returned more than it ever asked for.

Table of Contents

Table of Contents

Author's Note:

This is not my autobiography.

But it is a story shaped by things I've lived, felt, survived, and learned.

The protagonist is not me—she is a vessel. A mirror. A remix of truth and imagination.

Some moments are real. Some are reimagined. Some never happened exactly this way—but every emotion did.

PROLOGUE
THE SOUND OF SURVIVAL

Some people are named for the rhythm they'll carry their whole lives.

Cadence didn't know this when she was small, didn't understand that her name meant the rise and fall of music, the pattern of beats that keep a song moving forward even when the melody breaks.

She would learn, though. She would learn that life bends you in ways you never imagined... That it tests the tensile strength of your spirit, pulling and stretching until you're certain you'll snap. But bending is not breaking. Bending is survival.

Bending is the willow tree in the storm, the reed that touches the ground and springs back up.

This is a story about a girl who looked nothing like what she had gone through.

Who smiled when she wanted to scream. Who hummed melodies when the world went silent. Who learned that sometimes the only way to prove you're enough is to become more than anyone thought possible.

This is Cadence's story...

And it begins, as all stories do, with a breath... The first note of a song that would take thirty years to start to understand. Because time has a way of remixing your rhythm. Of turning lullabies into lessons, and heartbreak into harmony. Of teaching you that the beat doesn't stop just because the music changes. Sometimes it slows... sometimes it drops... sometimes it's nothing but the echo of your own pulse reminding you you're still here.

Cadence would learn to dance with silence. To make poetry out of pain and call it growth.

She would learn that healing isn't loud... It's a whisper that hums beneath the ribs, a quiet resurrection that no one claps for.

And when the world told her to stay in tempo, to follow the measure, to march instead of move... She would close her eyes and listen deeper to the rhythm beneath the rhythm. The one that belonged to her alone. Because some songs aren't written for applause. They're written to keep you alive. To remind you that your name is more than sound – it's survival set to melody.

So, when the curtain rises on the next verse of her life, she won't rush the tempo.

She'll breathe. She'll bend... And she'll remember that even broken chords can birth something beautiful, if you just keep living and playing...

PART ONE

ORIGINS OF RHYTHM

Chapter 1

Rain Before Memory

✦—✦

It started with rain.

Not the soft kind that hums on rooftops like a lullaby, but the kind that makes the sky feel heavy with memories. The kind that washes away the chalk lines of who you thought you were.

Cadence was two when she first heard the rhythm of her own name in a storm. She was in her crib, knees tucked to her chest, right before she stretched out and tested the strength of her vocal cords as lightning drew veins across the clouds in the Florida sky. Every strike felt like a heartbeat outside her own... loud, wild, unashamed, unapologetic.

Storms don't destroy. They cleanse. They make room for something green.

Cadence only saw the aftermath later – the puddles swallowing reflections, the silence that follows when thunder leaves the room. She didn't know then that life would mirror that storm. There would be seasons when she would lose herself in the downpour of doubt, where everything she built would feel too fragile to hold. She would also learn that nothing grows without rain.

The thing about losing your father at two years old is that you don't remember losing him. You just remember the absence, the negative space where a person should be. Cadence knew her father existed the way you know about distant countries... through photographs and other people's stories, through the shape of her own face in the mirror.

Florida, though – Florida she knew. Florida was real.

Florida was the upstairs apartment in Pompano Beach that felt like the whole world contained in the right-sized box. It was not luxury by anyone's standards except hers. When you are small, luxury is measured differently. It is measured in space and safety, in whether you have your own room and whether the weather makes you feel alive.

Cadence had her own room. So did her brother. So did her sister.

The apartment sprawled in that way childhood homes always do before you grow up and realize how small they actually were, each room holding its own universe of possibility. The weather was perfect – warm without being cruel, the kind of air that let her breathe easily. Her allergies, which would plague her later, stayed quiet in Florida like they understood this was cherished time that should not be disturbed.

Everything stayed quiet in Florida. At least, that is how memory painted it. Soft-edged. Golden.

They had toys. Not mountains of them, but enough. Her mother made sure of that, made sure they looked good even when money was tighter than she let on. Cadence didn't know about tight money then. She just knew that she felt safe. Her Florida cousins were close enough to see often, their laughter filling rooms and yards, their presence proof that fun could extend past the boundaries of who you lived with. When the sun set, it painted the sky in colors that made you believe in magic, and magic still felt possible because the world had not taught her otherwise yet.

Her mother seemed happy in Florida. Maybe she was just better at hiding the exhaustion. She worked the 8-to-5 at Vitas Healthcare, came home smelling like antiseptic and bottled sweet tea, hands scrubbed clean but somehow still carrying the weight of other people's emergencies.

When she walked through that door, there was a lightness in her that Cadence wouldn't see again for years. She would shelter them from the weight of the world, let them just be children, let them believe everything was fine because maybe, for a while, it was.

They would blast gospel music in the car with the windows down, volume turned up so high the bass vibrated through their bones. They would sing along like they were performing for stadiums instead of stuck in traffic. Those were good moments. Pure moments. The kind that made Cadence believe they had figured something out that other families were still searching for.

The family got along. Sure, siblings fought – it is what they do. There was more laughter than anger, though. More games than grudges. They were learning what their mother kept telling them: protect each other, don't let outsiders mess with any of you. In their own chaotic, childish way, they were trying. That is all anyone can really ask of children who don't yet understand how fragile everything is.

Cadence felt safe. She felt home. She felt like the world was exactly the size it should be, and she fit perfectly inside it.

That feeling lived in her bones during those years, settled into her like a second skeleton she would carry long after Florida became a place she could only visit in memory or take a two-hour-plus trip to.

It was there on the perfect afternoon when the air was crisp and generous. Her brother and sister decided, without asking, that her training wheels had served their purpose long enough. They unscrewed them like they were liberating her from something she had outgrown without knowing it. Maybe they were.

"You got this," her brother said, which was practically a speech coming from him. She believed him because he was her brother and brothers didn't lie about things like this.

She did have it. Sort of.

She wobbled at first, legs pumping hard, everything in her body uncertain except the part that wanted to fly. Then something clicked. The rhythm found her the way rhythm always would. Suddenly she was moving down the sidewalk, wind whipping her face, heart pounding with pure, unfiltered joy that tasted like freedom and felt like proof that she could do hard things if she just kept moving.

"I did it!" she screamed. "I did it!"

Her brother grinned in that way that meant he was proud but would never say it out loud. Then he raised the stakes the way siblings do when they see you succeed at something.

"Okay, now try mine."

His bike was bigger. Too big, really. Her feet barely reached the pedals.

Cadence had never been good at knowing her limits – wouldn't learn that skill for years, maybe never. She climbed on anyway. She made it work. She always made it work, even when the odds were stacked against her, even when logic said she shouldn't be able to reach.

It was clumsy. Wild. She didn't fall, though. She pedaled until her brother stopped her, laughing, genuinely impressed by this little girl who refused to know what was too big for her.

"Alright," her sister said, rolling her eyes but smiling because even siblings who pretend not to care can't help being proud sometimes. "Now do mine."

Her sister's bike was massive. Adult-sized.

Cadence stared at it like it was a dare she had not agreed to but couldn’t back down from. Backing down meant admitting there were things she couldn’t do. She was not ready to admit that yet. She was eight years old and still believed in her own invincibility.

"I can't – "

"You can," her sister interrupted. Not mean. Just certain. The kind of certainty that makes you believe in yourself even when you probably shouldn't.

Cadence tried. What else do you do when someone believes in you like that?

On her tiptoes – barely – she reached the pedals. The seat was too high. The handlebars were nearly out of reach. She pushed off anyway. Somehow, impossibly, she got it moving. The bike lurched forward, wobbling like a dream that doesn't know if it wants to be real yet. She pedaled while the neighborhood kids cheered. Her siblings watched with something that looked like pride.

She was doing it. She was actually doing it.

The whole world was cheering for her. Everything was perfect except for one small problem.

She didn't know how to stop.

The bike picked up speed. The handlebars shook in her hands. The ground blurred beneath her. Up ahead, coming fast like the punchline to a joke she didn't get yet, was a bush.

Well, she thought in that split second before impact, this is gonna hurt.

It did. A little.

She crashed into the bush with a sound that was half crunch, half yelp. Leaves in her hair, scratches on her arms, the bike on top of her in a tangle of metal and limbs.

Then she heard it – laughter, cheering, clapping. Her brother was pulling the bike off her. Her sister was helping her up, brushing leaves from her shirt. They were proud. Actually, genuinely proud.

Cadence stood there, scratched and stunned and grinning so hard her face hurt. She felt invincible.

To her, this was what happiness tasted like. This was what belonging felt like.

This was home.

Chapter 2

The Shape of Absence

✦—✦

That apartment in Pompano held other moments too, quieter ones that lived in the spaces between the big memories.

There was an evening when her mother had a friend over. They sat in the living room talking in that low, easy way adults do when they think kids are not listening. Cadence was supposed to be in her room playing, but she was not. She was hovering, watching, waiting, because she wanted cuddles and sometimes wanting is enough of a reason to break the rules.

Her mother didn't notice when Cadence slipped into the room. Didn't notice when she climbed into her lap, small and quiet and determined. Didn't notice when Cadence started rocking them – gently, rhythmically, like a song without words – because her mother was mid-sentence and sometimes mothers can do multiple things at once without even realizing it.

She kept talking, one arm automatically wrapping around Cadence, holding her close. Rocking with her. The conversation continued, seamless, unbothered, like this was exactly where Cadence was supposed to be.

Until her mother finally looked down and realized what had happened.

"Wait – " she started, then burst out laughing. "Girl, when did you even – get outta my lap!"

She was laughing, though. Her friend was laughing. Cadence was giggling, delighted by her own stealth, by the fact that she had managed to sneak affection the way other kids sneak cookies.

"You are something else," her mother said, shaking her head but not letting go right away, holding on for just a few more seconds because even when she was pretending to be exasperated, the love was real. "My baby girl. Always my baby girl."

Cadence felt it then – the warmth of being loved. Of being hers.

Even when the world got hard, there was this. There would always be this.

Or so she thought.

Childhood is full of things you think will last forever that disappear before you understand they were temporary.

There was a man who used to be part of their lives. His name doesn't matter now because he became irrelevant the moment the truth came out the way it did. What matters is that Cadence thought he was her father. He was around. He smiled at her. He made her mother laugh in a way that felt rare and precious, like finding something valuable you didn't know you had lost.

Because no one told her otherwise, she assumed.

Children do that – they fill in the gaps with hope, construct entire narratives out of what they wish were true.

She was seven, maybe eight, old enough to love him and old enough to trust the shape of the family she thought they were building. Old enough to call him what she thought he was and mean it.

She was home the day everything shattered.

Very close to that same living room where she had stolen cuddles from her mother, where happiness had felt like a permanent condition.

It started with her mother's voice on the phone, sharp and angry, a tone Cadence had never remembered hearing before. She was in the kitchen doing homework when it cut through the apartment like a blade.

"WHAT DO YOU MEAN?"

The tone made Cadence look up. Her mother never yelled like that. Not at them, not at anyone.

"And you wait until NOW to tell me? How long has this been – " Her mother's voice cracked. "Don't you lie to me. Don't you DARE – "

Cadence stood up. Walked toward the hallway. The bedroom door was cracked open, just enough to see her mother pacing, phone pressed so hard against her ear it had to have hurt.

"So, you've just been lying? This whole goddamn time?"

Cadence froze in the hallway.

Her mother didn't curse. Ever.

Church three times a week, grace before every meal, gospel music in the car turned up so loud you could feel the Holy Spirit in your chest – her mother didn't talk like that. Didn't use language that tasted bitter and wrong, fundamentally changing the atmosphere of a space that was supposed to be safe.

"You really wasted my time." Her mother's voice went high and broken, a sound Cadence had never heard before and hoped she would never hear again. "You told me you were – "

Silence. Whatever came through the phone made her mother sit down hard on the bed, like her legs had given out, like gravity had increased just for her.

"So, it was never – " More silence. Cadence could hear her mother breathing, could hear it catch and stutter. "I can't – I can't do this."

The phone hit the nightstand with a crack that made Cadence flinch.

Then the crying started.

It was not the quiet type of crying. Not the kind you can muffle with a pillow or hide behind closed doors. It was the kind that shook her whole body. The kind that sounded like drowning. The kind that meant something had been ripped away that she couldn't get back with apologies or time or anything else.

Cadence wanted to move closer to her. She wanted to go in there, fix it, make it stop, be enough to make her mother stop hurting. Before she could decide what eight-year-olds are supposed to do when their mothers break, the bedroom door slammed shut.

The sound echoed through the apartment, through Cadence's chest, through the rest of her childhood.

She stood in the hallway, same clothes still on from school, pencil still in her hand, listening to her mother cry through the wall. She understood – without understanding any of the words – that something fundamental had just changed. The world she thought she knew was being rewritten in real time. She didn't get a say in the edits.

Later – she didn't remember how much later, time does strange things when you are in shock – her mother sat her down. Told her the truth with eyes that were still red and a voice that was trying to be steady but kept fracturing at the edges.

"He's not your father, baby. Your real father... he's gone. He's been gone for a long time now."

Cadence nodded. She didn't cry. She didn't ask questions. She just absorbed it the way children absorb natural catastrophic events, internalizing the damage without understanding how to repair it.

Something hardened in her that day. Something that would stay hard for a long time. A vow formed itself in her chest, silent and absolute, carved into her ribs where she would carry it like a second skeleton.

No one will hurt my mother like this again. Not if I can stop it.

I will make something of myself. For her. For me. For everyone who ever thought we weren't enough.

She was only eight years old and she had just made a promise to a future she couldn't see yet.

Chapter 3

Leaving the Weather

✦ — ✦

Time moved the way it does when you are young – both fast and slow, both forgettable and unforgettable.

Cadence didn't know how much time passed between the door slamming and what came next. Days blurred into weeks... time blurred into a version of normal that didn't feel normal anymore.

What she did know was that one day, probably not long after the revelation but long enough that she had started to believe life might settle back into its rhythm, her mother sat them all down with that look on her face – the one that meant her mind was already made up, so don't bother arguing.

"We're moving," she said.

The words landed in the room like stones in water, creating ripples that would spread wider than any of them understood.

"To Texas."

Texas...

That word felt foreign in Cadence's mouth, sharp-edged and wrong, nothing like Florida which was soft and familiar and hers.

Cadence's stomach dropped. "What?"

"There's a hurricane coming," her mother continued, as if natural disasters were reason enough to uproot everything. "A bad one. I got a message from the Lord. We need to go."

The Lord. It was always the Lord when her mother needed backup for a decision that didn't make sense to anyone else.

"But – what about school? What about my friends? What about – "

"It's already decided."

"Ugghhh... When?"

"In two weeks. I'm sending you all up on a Greyhound with your aunty. I have a few things to finish up, but I'll be coming right behind you. We're going to stay with family until we get settled."

Something cracked inside Cadence. Not broke – not yet. Cracked. The first fracture in the foundation of her world.

She hated the idea. Hated it with the kind of fury only an eight-year-old can muster when everything they know is being ripped away without explanation, without permission, without any regard for the life they were building in their own small way.

"Ma, but I don't want to – "

"It's not about what you want, Cadence. It's about me doing what’s best for this family."

Her brother was staring at his plate. Her sister had her arms crossed and her jaw tight. Nobody was arguing because they all knew that it didn’t matter. Her mother had made a decision, and she was not changing it. The message from the Lord had been received. What did Greg O'Quin say in his song “I Told the Storm”? “... When God speaks... You have to cease.”

When the Lord speaks, you don’t get a vote.

"Can I at least – "

"No. Give me a few and I’ll be in there to help you pack your things."

That was it.

Conversation over.

Florida over.

Cadence went to her room and closed the door. She felt unheard. Silenced. That specific, suffocating feeling of being powerless in your own life – it would stay with her for years, teaching her to shrink herself, to tuck her wants behind her tongue and to become fluent in silence.

The Greyhound bus smelled like diesel and strangers and something Cadence couldn't name but would later recognize as loss.

She sat by the window. Her aunty beside her making small talk that Cadence couldn't bring herself to return. She watched Florida disappear in reverse. The trees she had climbed or wanted to climb. The familiar streets she knew by heart. The sky that had always felt like hers.

All of it melting into distance, becoming memory before she was ready to let it go, before she understood that some things you lose you never get back no matter how hard you try.

The ride felt like forever, every mile stretching into eternity the way time does when you are trapped in transition.

She thought about Texas the way kids think about things they don't understand – through stereotypes and half-formed ideas cobbled together from movies and ignorance. Cowboys. Horses. Dirt roads instead of pavement. Tumbleweeds rolling past wooden saloons. Everyone in cowboy boots and cowboy hats, talking slow and southern about things she wouldn't understand.

She was ignorant. She knew it. The fear was real anyway because fear doesn't care about facts.

What if Texas changed things in a way that could never be undone? What if it was hot and dusty and awful? What if she never fit in? What if her mother didn't come? What if something happened and Cadence was stuck in this strange place with people she barely knew, waiting for a mother who never arrived?

She pressed her forehead against the window and let the fear hum beneath her ribs like a song she didn't want to learn. She watched her piece of America blur past in shades of unknown.

When the bus finally pulled into the Dallas bus station around 2 PM, the heat hit her first.

Not Florida hot – Florida hot was humid, lush and thick, the kind of heat that wrapped around you like a blanket. Texas hot was dry and relentless, the kind that made you feel sticky and exposed, like the air itself was judging you for sweating.

The second thing she noticed, though, the thing that gave her a tiny spark of relief in the middle of all that displacement, was the pavement. Real pavement. Cars. Like, actual cars, not just horses.

At least that stereotype had been wrong. At least Texas had that much in common with civilization.

Her aunty was waiting by a brown Oldsmobile, waving. Three cousins in the back seat staring at her like she was a science experiment they weren't sure would work.

"How was the ride, baby?"

"Long."

They drove through streets that looked nothing like Pompano. Strip malls. Churches every three blocks. Everything flat and spread out like the city gave up on trying to be compact. No ocean. No palm trees swaying in the breeze. Just concrete, asphalt, sky, and heat that made the air shimmer.

Her aunty and uncle's apartment had dark brown brick. There was no yard, but developers tried to make up for it with a community pool.

Three kids already lived there. Now three more.

"Y'all gonna share the back room," her aunty said, pointing.

The room had two twin bunk beds and a dresser. There were also plastic bins for the three of them.

Cadence's suitcases fit in the closet. Barely.

Through the window she could see the neighborhood parking lot. Dirt patches where concrete should be. Plastic chairs on some people's patios. A dog barking somewhere in the distance.

This was not Florida.

This was not even close.

Her mother came, eventually. She had promised she would and she did, because her mother always kept her promises even when everything else was falling apart.

Something had shifted, though. Something had been left behind in Florida that they would never get back, some essential piece of who they were as a family before Texas, before the hurricane, before the message from the Lord that changed everything.

Cadence still didn't have the words for it. She didn't know how to say: I feel like I lost something I didn't even know I had.

She just tucked it away, added it to the growing pile of feelings she didn't know what to do with, feelings that would eventually need somewhere to go but for now just lived inside her chest like extra ribs that were out of place.

Life in Texas had begun.

The Greyhound bus ride was not just a trip between states. It was a threshold. The moment when childhood stopped being something that just happened to her and started being something she had to survive.

The storm was not punishment. It was prophecy, preparing her for all the other storms that would come.

Cadence – named for rhythm, for the rise and fall of music, for the pattern that keeps a song moving even when the melody breaks – was just beginning to learn what bending really meant.

REFLECTION ONE

Before the dust, there was only the rain—

A Florida sky that knew her by name.

The rhythm of safety, a world in a box,

The turn of a key, the absence of locks.

But the melody shifted, the bass grew too deep,

A vow was a secret she promised to keep.

Leaving the weather, she boarded the bus,

Exchanging the "me" for a crowded "us".

A Greyhound bridge between palm trees and heat,

The first broken chord of a life bittersweet.

PART TWO

LEARNING TO BEND

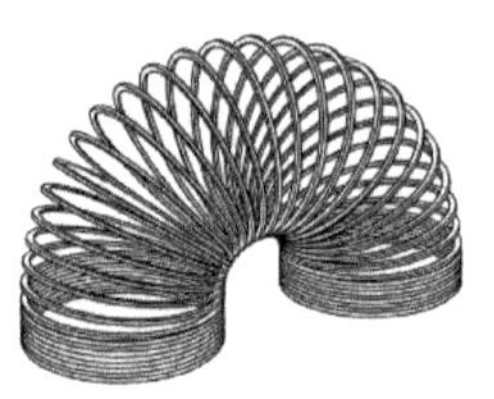

Chapter 4

Temporary Homes

✦—✦

Texas didn't feel like home, but that is the thing about being nine years old – you learn to adapt faster than you want to, faster than you should have to.

Her aunty and uncle's house was full in a way that felt both overwhelming and comforting. Six kids in total crammed into spaces that weren't designed for that many bodies, that many voices, that many needs competing for attention. Cadence shared everything – space, toys, attention, the bathroom in the mornings when everyone was trying to get ready all at once. She knew how to handle things when it was just her and her siblings. Now, time was a little more tricky. It was not what she wanted. It was what she had. She was quickly learning that sometimes those are not the same thing.

Her cousins made it bearable. Better than bearable, actually. They got close in the kind of way that kids do when they are thrown together and told to make it work – playing card games until someone accused someone else of cheating, collecting cards like they were currency, trading them like Wall Street brokers making deals that felt important even when they really weren't. They would sneak out to explore parts of the city they weren't supposed to see, walking through neighborhoods and corporate garages that felt foreign and familiar at the same time, testing the boundaries of what they could get away with while their parents were busy just trying to keep everyone fed, clothed, and alive.

It was temporary, though. Everything was temporary now.

A couple of months – maybe more, maybe less, time moved strangely during that period – and then her mother found them a place. A townhome in Garland that felt like a new challenge to take on. The feeling was still novel and fresh so she felt like maybe they could rebuild what they had lost in Florida. Maybe they could at least build something new that didn't hurt as much to look at.

Everyone got their own room again, which felt very satisfying after months of shared space, and after learning to fall asleep with other people's breathing filling the air. Cadence claimed her room the way you claim territory, spreading out in it, testing its dimensions, making it hers in the way only a kid who has lost ownership of space could understand. Best of all, it was next door to her mother's room.

The townhome was nice. Nicer than it probably was objectively. When you are measuring against loss and displacement, nice is very relative. It helped create memories that made her temporarily forget about missing Florida, moments that existed in their own right instead of as comparisons to what came before. It felt like getting their lives back, like maybe this Texas thing might work after all.

Cadence was older now, though. More aware. Awareness is both a gift and a curse when you are still too young to do anything with the information it gives you.

She noticed her mother's absence more. Not physically – her mother was there, still working as a nurse at Vitas Healthcare, still coming home at the end of long 8-to-5 shifts. The absence she felt was emotional. The lightness that had existed in Florida, that ease that made everything feel manageable, had been replaced by something heavier. Exhaustion, maybe. The weight of doing it all alone in a place that was not home, without the support system they had left behind.

Her mother was trying, she always tried. However, the trying looked different now. More strained. More like survival and less like living.

She noticed her siblings getting into more trouble too, testing boundaries in ways they had not before. They were acting out in ways that seemed designed to get attention even if it was negative attention. Their mother, who used to be more strict about grades and behavior, had transformed into someone more lenient.

"Do better next time," she would say when report cards came home with grades that should have warranted a whooping or a stricter response.

Not because she didn't care, but because she was running on empty and had to choose her battles. Sometimes the battles you choose are the ones based on continuity rather than excellence.

Around this time, Cadence's sister started going to one of their older cousin's houses on weekends, seeking refuge in a space that was not crowded with siblings and disarray. They had a music room there – a safe haven that was painted in a deep red like the inside of a heartbeat, with velvet recliners that swallowed you whole in the best way.

When you sat in that room with the music playing, it wrapped around you like comfort itself, making you forget about the world waiting on the other side of the door. It was a solemn space, the kind you need when you are trying to figure out who you are separate from everyone who thinks they know you.

Once Cadence and her brother discovered how nice it was, they wanted in. They started showing up on weekends too, claiming space in the deep red room, sinking into those velvet recliners, letting the music do what music does when you let it – transports you somewhere that makes undesired emotions disappear.

Their sister's sanctuary became shared territory. The more they invaded it, the less she came. It stopped being her safe place because nothing stays sacred when everyone knows about it and when everyone wants a piece of what made you feel whole.

Something else was happening in that house, though. Something Cadence didn't fully recognize yet but would later recognize as pivotal.

Brandon – their older cousin, the one who seemed to have figured something out about life that everyone else was still struggling with – started paying attention to them and their other cousins in a different way. Not just as kids to tolerate but as people worth investing in. He would incentivize them to do better in school, in life in general, offering rewards for grades and effort in a way their mother no longer had the energy to do.

He didn't live in the clearance section like everyone else seemed to. Didn't scramble for the basics. He lived life and was able to afford it.

Cadence noticed. She kept an eye on that difference, filing it away for later, for when she would be old enough to understand what it meant and how to get there herself.

Chapter 5

Lessons That Stayed

✦—✦

School in Texas was different from school in Florida in a manner that Cadence couldn't quite articulate but that she felt deeply.

She was too young to understand the difference between good schools and bad schools, between resourced and under-resourced, between neighborhoods that invested in education and neighborhoods that were just trying to keep the lights on. She just knew she didn't like many of her schools because she felt that something was missing even if she couldn't name what.

There were a few teachers who stood out, though. Those who were strict in the way that actually meant they cared, who demanded excellence not because they were mean, but because they believed their students were capable of it.

Ms. Moses was one of those teachers.

Third grade. She was strict – not the kind of strict that crushes spirits but the kind that shapes them. The kind that pushes you because she sees something in you that you don't see in yourself yet.

She would throw things in class – it wasn't to hurt anyone, but it helped to keep them entertained, to keep attention from wandering, to make learning feel alive instead of like something you had to endure. She would trade classroom chores for candy, turning the mundane into transactions that felt important. After lunch, or sometimes at the start of the day, you had to solve math problems just to make it into the classroom, turning entry into an achievement.

She made learning fun in a way Cadence had not experienced before, made it feel like a game you could win if you just paid attention and tried.

Cadence had never been great at taking tests – something about the pressure, the time limits, the way questions were phrased made her brain freeze up in ways it didn't during normal learning. That year she was slated to take her first standardized state test, one of those exams that is supposed to measure whether you are learning what you should be learning, whether you are keeping up with kids in other places who have different lives and different resources.

Ms. Moses made her a bet.

If Cadence passed the test – no matter how long it took, no matter what the score was, just passed – Ms. Moses would do a cartwheel. A full cartwheel, right in front of her in the hallway.

Cadence took that bet seriously because it felt like Ms. Moses believed in her in a way that was tangible, that if she won the bet it would be more than just a success... it would be proof that she could actually do anything that she put her mind to and actions behind.

She took that test, worked through every problem even when her brain wanted to give up, even when the clock kept ticking and other kids finished and left and she was still there, still trying.

She was the last person to finish.

She passed.

Ms. Moses, true to her word, did a cartwheel. Right there in the hallway, limbs flying, Cadence cheering and grinning so hard her face hurt because someone had believed in her enough to make a ridiculous promise and keep it. Her mother just watched in amusement.

That moment lived in her head, rent free, for years afterward, a reminder that people could surprise you, that belief could be shown in weird ways, and that sometimes the smallest gestures mean everything.

Fourth grade brought something else – a different kind of lesson that had nothing to do with math problems or standardized tests.

There was a boy at church, always in his wheelchair, always smiling in a way that made you feel like everything would be okay even when you knew it wouldn't. He was very pleasant to be around, the kind of person everyone genuinely loved without having to try, without the performance that usually comes with being well-liked.

Cadence would see him on Sundays, interact with him the way kids do –

simple conversations, shared jokes, the comfortable routine of familiar faces in familiar places.

There had been talks. Grown-up whispers that tried to prepare everyone for what was coming, conversations in hushed tones about how he was not going to last much longer. Kids don't really understand that kind of preparation, though. Don't know how to hold space for future grief when the person is still there, still smiling, still present.

One Sunday she saw him and they interacted as normal. She didn't know it would be the last time. Didn't know to memorize the moment, to hold onto it tighter, to say something more meaningful than whatever casual thing she probably said.

The next time she came to church, he was not there.

Someone – she didn't remember who, didn't remember the exact words – told her that he had fulfilled his purpose on earth and was now in heaven with the angels. The same language they had used about her father, the same soft explanation meant to cushion the blow of permanent absence.

She was sad. She was happy too, in that complicated way you can be when someone's suffering is over but you still miss them. She missed him. Missed seeing him there, missed that smile, missed the casual normalcy of his presence.

Something clicked into place that had not before. Death was not abstract anymore, was not just a concept people explained in careful voices. Death meant no return to earth. Life would continue – it had to continue – but the people you lost couldn't continue the journey with you. They couldn't grow up alongside you, couldn't be there for the next Sunday or the one after that. They had to become something else.

Guiding angels, the grown-ups said. Watching from heaven, they said.

Maybe that was true, maybe it was not. Either way they were gone in a way that made gone feel heavier than it ever had felt before.

It made her think about her father differently. Not just as an absence she had never really known, but as a person who would have continued if he could have. Who would have been there for bike rides and talent shows and moving to Texas. Who would have aged while she aged, changed while she changed.

He couldn't, though. The same way this boy couldn't. The same way anyone who died couldn't, no matter how much people loved them or needed them to stay.

Making friends in Texas was easier than Cadence expected after that, maybe because she understood now that time with people mattered in ways she had not fully grasped before.

Chapter 6

What We Chase

✦ — ✦

When they moved to the townhome, exploring became a thing again. Not the same as the aunty and uncle's neighborhood kind, but similar enough that it was not so peculiar.

She and her brother would venture out into Garland, mapping territory the way kids do when they are trying to understand the geography of their new lives. They found forgotten gadgets under bridges – old toys, broken electronics, pieces of other people's lives left behind. They found wasp nests and learned to give them wide berth, learned which shortcuts were worth the risk and which ones would get you stung. They found other people's playgrounds in other neighborhoods, claimed them temporarily like pirates claiming islands, playing until someone or the street lights told them to go home or until boredom sent them searching for the next discovery.

Then there was the day of the cats.

Cadence was not sure what happened – some sort of ecological event she didn't have the vocabulary to explain – but one afternoon as the sun was setting, there was a sudden influx of baby kittens that seemed to have taken over the complex like an invasion from a movie she had watched but couldn't remember the name of. They were everywhere. Under cars, in bushes, darting across sidewalks with that frantic kitten energy that makes them seem like they are vibrating at a different frequency than the rest of the world.

She locked eyes with one.

It was small and scrappy and probably feral, probably terrified, probably had no interest whatsoever in being caught by a nine-year-old girl with determination in her eyes and no real plan beyond *I want that cat*.

Cadence didn't care about logistics. She just knew she wanted it, needed it, had to have it in the way you know things when you are young, and desire is simple and absolute.

She took off running.

The kitten took off too, and the chase commenced like something choreographed by chaos itself. Through bushes that scratched her arms and caught her clothes. Under the underpass where the light got weird and sounds echoed. Back up onto the main street where kids on their bikes had to swerve and probably cursed thinking they were cool. Under vehicles where she had to get low, had to believe in her own invincibility to crawl into spaces that could collapse or drive away.

She was focused the way predators are focused, the way nothing else exists except the thing you are chasing and the belief that you will catch it if you just don't give up.

Then, finally, she got a hold of the tail.

She pulled it close enough to grab the body, close enough to wrap her arms around it in a hug that was probably too tight, that definitely made the kitten panic. She held it like Hugo the Abominable Snowman from Looney Tunes – "I will love him and pet him and squeeze him" – while the kitten thrashed and scratched and made it very clear this was not consensual affection.

Cadence didn't care about the scratches multiplying on her arms. She had gone through too much to get this cat. This was hers now.

Her siblings found her there, scratched up and grinning, holding a terrified kitten that wanted nothing to do with her love. Because they recognized the hustle, recognized the determination it took to want something that bad and actually go get it, they helped. They formed a united front and talked their mother into letting her keep it, made the case that Cadence had earned this, that the scratches were proof of commitment.

Their mother said yes. Reluctant yes, maybe. Resigned yes. Yes.

Cadence had her cat.

During these years – third, fourth, fifth grade – her mother was still herself in a lot of ways. Still a nurse, still working the long 8-to-5 shifts that nursing demands. When she was home, really home, she was happy. Outgoing. Fun in the way she had been in Florida, or close enough that Cadence could pretend nothing had fundamentally changed.

They would exercise together, turning the living room into a makeshift gym, dancing to routines they made up as they went. They would go out to shop and watch movies, have normal mother-daughter time that felt like affluence when you measured it against all the time they didn't have.

There were cracks too, though.

Her mother started dating again – tentatively, carefully, the way people date when they have been hurt before and are trying not to repeat patterns. Cadence didn't trust the new guy. Cadence didn't trust any guy, really, because the wound from before was still fresh even if no one talked about it anymore. The man who was not her father had taught her something about trust and how easily it breaks, and she carried that lesson into every new relationship her mother attempted.

She would watch them with eyes that were too suspicious for a kid her age, looking for signs of the hurt that would inevitably come, preparing herself to protect her mother even though she was still too small to actually protect anyone from anything real.

Fifth grade brought stories that are fun to think back on. For instance, there was the talent show.

One of those moments that would crystallize into the kind of memory that makes you cringe years later but also teaches you something about failure and recovery. Cadence had agreed to perform with one of her best friends and her sister – a whole routine they had practiced until it was perfect. The choreography was tight. The lyrics memorized. The transitions smooth. They had it down, could do it in their sleep, could probably do it under pressure.

Except pressure turned out to be different than practice.

Showtime came. Cadence walked onto that stage with confidence that evaporated the second she saw all those faces looking at her. She had gotten through most of the song. Then when her solo came up, she froze. Not just forgot-a-line froze but full-body, brain-shutdown, cannot-remember-how-to-breathe froze.

She choked. Completely and utterly choked.

Then, because standing there frozen felt worse than running, she ran off the stage in embarrassment that burned through her like fire.

Her friends finished the routine without her. The audience probably didn't even notice, or if they did, they were kind enough not to make a big deal of it. Somehow – somehow – they still made top three for the prizes.

Which should have felt like a win but mostly felt like proof that she had let everyone down and they had succeeded despite her, not because of her.

The lesson was not about talent or preparation. It was about pressure and fear and the gap between knowing you can do something and actually doing it when it matters. About how your body can betray you even when your mind knows better. About how failure feels when you are nine years old and convinced everyone will remember this forever even though, realistically, most people forgot about it by lunch the next day.

Cadence didn't forget, though. She carried that moment like a stone in her pocket, a reminder that confidence without follow-through is just noise, that wanting to be good at something is not the same as being good at it, that sometimes you are your own worst enemy.

She wouldn't choke like that again. Not if she could help it.

REFLECTION TWO

Four walls are a shell, but a room is a skin,

A place to keep out all the noise that got in.

She learned how to measure the gaps in the day,

To tuck all her "wantings" and "wishings" away.

The red room was velvet, a heartbeat of song,

A sanctuary where she finally belonged.

But even the sacred is eventually shared,

And silence is heavy for those who are scared.

She watched the horizon, she looked for the sign,

Between survival and life, she was drawing the line.

PART THREE

THE NOISE YEARS

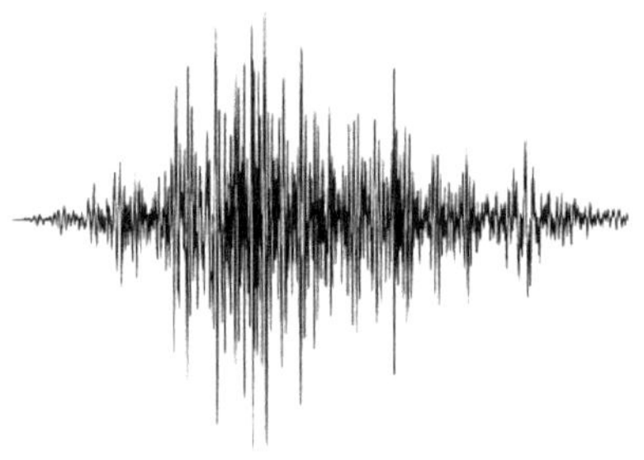

Chapter 7

Always the New Girl

✦ — ✦

Seventh and eighth grade were cool. Cadence had not experienced the continuity of staying at the same school for more than a year since Florida.

She was able to stay at the same school since they didn't have to move to a different place in Dallas. She was afforded the enjoyment of the same rhythm that let her breathe without wondering what would change next. That stability was temporary, though. Somewhere deep down she knew it even while she was living it. Her mother was always looking for something different, something better, something that might finally feel like the right fit.

Freshman year shattered the pattern she had just gotten used to.

They moved to Seagoville, a nice new house in a place that felt simultaneously closer and further from everything that mattered. New school. New neighborhood. New set of rules about where you could walk and who you could trust. Cadence adjusted the way she had learned to adjust – quickly, quietly, making it look easy even when it was not.

Sophomore year was in this same house, but now just another different school. Another year of building something from nothing. This school was like a nightmare that had come to life. The only silver lining was that it was within walking distance of her house, and her older brother also went to the same school.

Junior year arrived and they were moving, AGAIN! Back to Garland this time, back to a place that should have felt like returning but instead felt like starting over. Places looked familiar, but she had only known them when she was a different version of herself. Now she was at yet another school. She had another set of faces to memorize. Another first day where she had to reintroduce herself all while trying to figure out where she would fit in.

I need to get out of here.

This thought started appearing somewhere in the middle of all that moving, maybe during the Seagoville years, maybe earlier. It wasn't loud or dramatic, though. Just a quiet realization that kept surfacing whenever boxes got packed, whenever her mother announced another fresh start, or whenever Cadence had to walk into another classroom full of kids who already had their friend groups established, and their inside jokes figured out.

Home during those years was not refuge. It was noise.

There were constant arguments where no one wanted to listen to each other, but where everyone just wanted to be heard and nobody knew how to make space for anyone else's voice. Someone was always yelling at someone else about something – responsibilities not being done, attitudes not appreciated, space invaded, boundaries crossed, etc. It was draining in a way that made exhaustion feel like a permanent condition. Frustrating in a way that made peace feel like a privilege that only other people got to experience.

Cadence didn’t have direction living there. There was not much guidance either, outside of the typical: stay out of trouble. She just had chaos and the expectation that she would figure it out on her own while navigating everyone else's chaos too.

There was another house, though.

Brandon's house.

That house felt like stepping into a different reality.

Chapter 8

Another House, Another Way

✦—✦

It started as occasional visits, those quickly became frequent escapes, and those then transitioned into her default destination whenever home got to be too much.

Brandon's house was where you went when you needed to remember that life could be different. It was big enough for lots of people without feeling crowded. It had game stations and a game room where you could lose yourself in virtual worlds that made more sense than the real one.

Another thing that made his place different was that on the way back from running errands they would get fast food. Brandon would try and teach them how to make decisions since most of their decisions would be made for them. So, on the weekends they would get taken to actual restaurants where you sat down and ordered what you wanted and didn't have to worry about the bill.

It was fun there. The simple, uncomplicated type of fun that didn't come with arguments, high levels of stress, or the weight of being torn at home.

Cadence started hanging around more during the eighth, ninth, and tenth grade, and started noticing things she hadn't paid attention to before.

The way Brandon worked from home, which was unusual back then, years before COVID made it normal. She would see him disappear into his office, see the glow of computer screens through the doorway, and hear the occasional phone call where he sounded professional and in charge of what was going on.

So, naturally, she got curious. She started peeking her head into his office while he worked, lingering in the doorway until he noticed her.

"What do you do?" she would ask.

"You wouldn't understand," he would say, not meanly, just matter-of-factly.

That never stopped her though.

She kept asking. Kept showing up. Kept being curious in a way that was persistent enough that eventually he started trying to explain things. Despite thinking that she probably wouldn't fully grasp the concepts of what he explained, he still tried. It became a rhythm between them – her asking, him attempting to translate his world into language she could comprehend. But the both of them knew that the full understanding wasn't the point. The trying was the point.

She was noticing other things too. The way he lived his life. The peace in his house even when it was full of people. Whatever occurred within the island of him and his wife's room remained a total mystery, as if the space were vacuum-sealed; no matter the storm inside, it never leaked, bled, or spilled over into the rest of the house or onto anyone else. They seemed happy. They didn't seem to struggle. Didn't seem to stress about money or bills or whether they could afford to take everyone out to dinner.

She had aunts and uncles who lived like this too. People who had figured out some formula that made life look easy instead of exhausting. Watching them, being around them, made something sprout and crystallize in Cadence's mind.

She didn't want to struggle.

She didn't want life to be a constant scramble. Didn't want to spend her adulthood the way she had seen other adults spending it – working hard but never getting ahead, moving frequently but never landing somewhere that stuck.

Music was her outlet during these years, the place where all the feelings she couldn't say out loud in the turbulence got reformed into something that made sense.

She wrote constantly, pouring everything into songs – the frustration, the exhaustion, the longing for something different, the confusion about who she was becoming. She thought about Fantasia Barrino, who wrote about her life experiences and turned her struggle into art. That is what Cadence inadvertently began to do. She turned all of this – the moving, the arguments, the feeling of being stuck – into songs that might matter to someone, somewhere. Even if it didn't, it mattered enough to her.

She was hoping for a record deal. Dreaming about it in the way teenagers dream about escape routes that looked like a way out. If she could just get someone to hear her music, to recognize that she had something worth listening to, then everything would change. The struggle would become a shadow in the background of the rest of her life. The mess would become the before that made the after meaningful.

She didn't know yet that music wouldn't be her way out.

She needed to believe it was, though. Needed something to aim for that felt bigger than just surviving another move, another school, another year of noise.

Chapter 9

Choosing Quiet

✦ — ✦

Junior year in Garland should have felt like an achievement being back in a place she knew, back near Brandon's house, and where she could escape more easily.

It just felt like another iteration of the same pattern.

Near the end of junior year, her mother started making those similar sounds again. The ones that meant she was getting restless looking at listings and talking about fresh starts.

They were going to move. Again!

Cadence was tired!

Tired of changing schools! Tired of being the new kid! Tired of building something only to have it disrupted before it could become something worth having! She was especially tired at the thought of changing schools for senior year – the year that was supposed to be about finishing strong and about having memories with people you had known for more than a few months.

She was already spending most of her free time at Brandon's house anyway. Using it as an escape, as a place where she could do stuff without the thought of getting on someone's nerves. Her cousins – the two sisters who were seniors while she was a junior – were there, and being around them felt easier than being home with her siblings.

Someone made a joke. Maybe Brandon, maybe one of her other cousins. She couldn't remember later who said it first.

The joke was: "Why don't you just move in? Finish your senior year at the same school so you don't have to adjust anymore."

It was said casually. Lightly. The way you joke about things that might be slightly serious underneath the humor.

Cadence laughed.

The idea lodged itself in her mind, though, and wouldn't leave.

She really thought about it. More frequently as her junior year hit the mid-point mark.

About what it would mean to stay at the same school to finish out her senior year. About not having to be the new kid again. About living in the house that felt like placidity instead of an emotional prison. About having some sense of stability back.

Also, though, about leaving her mother. Leaving her siblings. Becoming the kid who moved out before she graduated high school. The guilt was immediate and heavy.

She held off on the idea as long as she could, let it sit in the category of things we joked about but won't actually do. But her mother kept talking about moving. Kept looking at places. The joke kept sounding less like a joke and more like something that was becoming a consideration.

Until one day her mother looked at her and said something that changed everything.

"It might be a good idea to start getting some things together. Have you thought about when you were going to start moving your stuff over to Brandon's?"

Time seemed to have sped up so fast that Cadence was not really ready for the conversation. She had to give an answer, though. It was now presented as an option they needed to discuss. Her mother had already pretty much made the decision. Maybe she had heard the longing underneath all the jokes and was giving Cadence permission to want something different.

Cadence was in shock. She was excited, but also nervous in a way that made her stomach tight.

This was big. This was very different. This was admitting that home was not working, that she needed something her mother couldn't provide, that at seventeen she was choosing a different path than the one her family was walking.

So, she started packing. She started carrying her things over to Brandon's house little by little. Her clothes. Her music equipment. The pieces of herself that she needed in order to rebuild herself in comfort in her new space.

Moving out before eighteen felt like crossing a horizon she couldn't uncross. Like making a statement about who she was and what she needed that would echo through the rest of her relationships with her family. She felt guilt for leaving. Relief for having somewhere to go. Gratitude that Brandon and his wife had said yes without hesitation. But lots of grief for the version of family she had wanted but would never really have.

The last box she carried over contained her notebooks. Years of lyrics, years of feelings she couldn't say vocally, years of trying to make sense of a life that kept changing shape before she could figure out how to hold it.

Dropping the boxes into the quiet of the new room, she felt an internal tectonic shift.

She wasn't 'fixed' – the cracks were all still there – but she wasn't falling apart anymore

She was just... recalibrated.

She was seventeen years old. She had just made a decision that felt both selfish and necessary, and it was both freeing and terrifying.

She sat on the edge of the bed that would be hers for the years to come and let herself breathe without having no choice but to be listening to arguments through the walls. She was able to exhale without wondering when the next announcement would come, or without bracing for the ground to readjust beneath her again.

For the first time in years, the quiet didn't feel temporary.

It felt like achievability.

REFLECTION THREE

Junior year shadows and restlessness growing,

The weight of the staying, the fear of the going.

She stood at the threshold of seventeen's door,

Unable to carry the "less" anymore.

To leave was a fracture, a guilt-ridden choice,

But only in quiet could she find her own voice.

A move to a mentor, a shift in the beat,

The sound of the cycle admitting defeat.

PART FOUR

REWRITING THE MEASURE

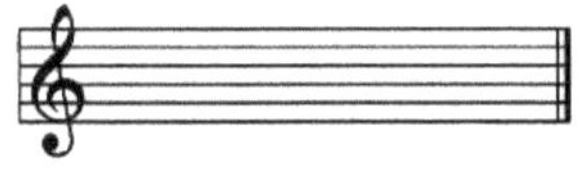

Chapter 10

Structure and Silence

✦—✦

Living with Brandon meant living with structure.

Daily life was different. There was more silence and more predictability. Brandon treated all the kids in the house inclusively, and it was felt. He did his best not to treat anyone more special than the next person, even though obviously his daughter got treated differently because she was actually his and he had to. Cadence respected that, understood it, didn't take it personally at all.

Brandon was viewed as the father figure with additional kids that he didn't ask for but took very good care of. Cadence just so happened to become one of those bonus kids.

His wife treated all the kids the same – that can be a story for another time – but she did well with ensuring that you could explicitly tell who was who by who she gave special treatment to. Expected, reasonable. That was fine. Her mother was cordial. They respected each other without needing to bond too much. It was enough.

The two cousin sisters who had been seniors when Cadence was a junior had become her close friends through proximity and shared experience. They did lots of stuff together, preferred togetherness over solo adventures. That is how Cadence's mother had raised her anyway – don't do stuff on your own, especially being young, black, and being a woman in America. She didn't mind. The comfort was in the presumed safety and there were always strength in numbers.

Cadence had chores and responsibilities, but they were simple: take care of yourself and clean up after yourself. She occasionally took on side jobs to have extra money so that she could avoid asking for things she wanted but didn't necessarily need. After daylight savings, though, safety concerns at her workplace made everyone nervous. Since it was better to be safe than sorry, she quit before anything bad could happen, and before the opportunity for something dangerous even had the chance to present itself.

Her best friend from sophomore year had become something more. They had begun "talking" at the end of freshman year. He wanted to date but she was not really interested because she cared more about the friendship, and if things were to go awry she didn't want to lose her best friend. The both of them were settling into a friendship that felt safe because it didn't demand anything complicated, but junior year shifted something. Maybe it was the stability. Maybe it was the fact that she was living a different life now and needed something familiar to hold onto. Whatever the reason, when he asked again, she thought: why not?

He was her best friend. She trusted him. They went to different schools, which meant their relationship existed in the spaces between classes and on weekends, but that just made it feel manageable.

They had the rare opportunity to potentially attend two proms – one at his school's venue and the other at hers – because when you are dating someone from another school, you get to dress up and wear your formal wear twice. It would be double the fun, double the dancing, double the photos for their parents to embarrass them with later. They had no doubt that it would be a great time at both. Cadence felt almost like a regular teenager doing regular teenage things, which was a feeling she had been chasing without realizing it.

Music production had been happening in the background long before senior year arrived. Back in sophomore year, Brandon had recognized something in her – not just talent, but hunger. The way she consumed music, the way she talked about it, the way it seemed to be the language she thought in when speech went beyond the reach of an explanation and only a gesture or silence would suffice. He had introduced her to production and had given her her first DAW – digital audio workstation – essentially handing her the keys to a paradise she didn't even know had existed.

He wanted her to be a triple threat. A singer, writer, and a producer. At the time she had just been a singer and a writer. Production was the final piece of his formula for her and the thing that would make her complete as a musical artist.

After he taught her the basics, she practiced daily. Not because she had to, but because it felt like speaking a language that only she could translate. It started from within – some combination of emotion and intention with sound – and production was her way of bringing it outward, making the internal something tangible. She made beats for herself. It took a while to get decent, but then it just kept getting easier. Practice didn't make perfect, practice made happiness. It truly made her happy in a way that was pure and uncomplicated by expectation or external validation.

Her hierarchy was clear: singing was still top, then writing, then production. She loved all three, but that was the order they lived in inside of her heart during that time. She shared most of her music with Brandon and one of her other cousins, keeping it local to home and close to connection. Eventually she would post some to SoundCloud and Spotify, but for the longest time her audience was small and trusted.

Brandon kept talking to her about her future. Kept pushing conversations she was not sure she wanted to have because they required thinking past graduation and past the comfortable present where she could still pretend music would save her.

"What are you going to do after school?" he would ask.

Prior to those conversations, Cadence had assumed she would just graduate and start working, like everyone else she had seen do. Get a job. Make money. Figure it out as you go.

Brandon pushed. "You should go to college."

"I don't know," she would say.

"Apply anyway. See what happens."

And so, she did. Because looking at the bigger picture, he was the only person outside of teachers who was pushing for it and making it seem not just possible but expected. She submitted applications. Waited. Then the acceptance letters came – four of them, from actual universities, saying yes to her, saying you belong here, saying you are good enough for this.

Financial aid didn’t come through quickly enough, though. Reality had timing that didn’t align with dreams. She ended up at community college instead, which felt like a step down until she reframed it as still a step forward. She got loans. She got a job to help pay for school on top of the loans. It built character. She appreciated it even when appreciation felt like the consolation prize for not getting what she wanted.

Senior year in high school was when she knew she needed to figure out what came next. Brandon kept broadening her possibilities and kept instilling in her that she could *do* more and *be* more. Their conversations transformed from abstract to more realistic.

"If I don't break the cycle, who will?" she found herself saying, though she was not sure if she had thought it first or if Brandon had planted the seed so skillfully she thought it was hers.

Cadence would constantly initiate conversations about how she didn't want to end up like everyone else. She wanted to succeed. Brandon had made it vividly clear that success meant following the money until she had the financial freedom to follow her passion. Not the other way around. Not passion first and hope money follows. Money first. Security first.

Then passion gets to exist without the desperation that kills it.

College could open doors a regular high school diploma couldn't. That became clear through Brandon's patient explanations, through seeing how he and other accomplished people lived, and through understanding that education was infrastructure for a life worth having. A life worth having meant a life with sacrifice.

However, to be irrefutably clear, music was always in the back of her head as a backup, a hobby, or something that would have to wait until she made money... despite her wishing it could take center stage. The dream of a record deal was still there during senior year in high school, but it was slipping into the background, becoming quieter as reality got louder.

Just as her and her boyfriend had originally imagined, prom had now happened. They attended two proms, both fun, both feeling like the kind of memories you are supposed to make when you are seventeen and the world still feels like it is unfolding exactly as it should.

Unfortunately, after prom, Cadence found out that her boyfriend had been cheating on her. The betrayal was sharp and specific, the kind that makes you question whether you ever really knew the person you thought you knew best.

She broke up with him a few months before graduation. It hurt. The hurt gave her something to write about, finally. The writers block that had been hovering lifted temporarily due to pain that she had never felt before and hoped she would never have to feel again. Songs poured out the way they used to, charged with emotion that demanded to be shaped into something.

Then she worked on healing... but trauma from that kind of hurt from someone you thought you've fallen in love with would take a while to heal from completely.

With healing came the block again, stronger this time. She had become too content with her situation. Living with Brandon was peaceful and it made emotional songwriting difficult. She didn't have the disarray to process anymore. She didn't have the pain sharp enough to need transformation. When she tried to write anyway, it felt forced. Like she was manufacturing emotion instead of channeling it.

Chapter 11

The Long Way Through

✦ — ✦

College was not what she expected.

Not because it was harder academically – though it was – but because everything had to happen simultaneously. She couldn't just be a student. She had to be a student, an employee, a functioning adult, and someone who was trying to build a future while barely managing the present.

Being in college while working forty hours a week... sometimes more, was not the same level of difficulty for everyone alike. The schedule was relentless for her in a way that made sleep feel like an allowance and rest feel like something only other people got to experience. She would go to class, go to work, come home exhausted, and do homework until her eyes couldn't stay open anymore. Then she would sleep for a few hours, wake up, and do it all over again.

She learned code-switching without anyone teaching her explicitly. She had adapted and learned to be one version of herself where she worked during her internship – professional, polished, careful about how she spoke and what she revealed. Then, she learned to be another version at school. She was another version of herself at Brandon's house, and another version with her mother and siblings. The switching became automatic, necessary, and extremely socially exhausting.

She recognized that excellence was not just a goal but a strategy. So, she learned and she climbed from entry-level to mid-level positions in corporate environments that didn't always make space for people who looked like her. Being twice as good meant you might be considered almost equal. Showing up early and staying late was not optional if you wanted to be taken seriously.

Brandon kept teaching her things about money. He taught her more about investing and about thinking long-term to help prepare her for when the present felt overwhelming. He taught her about being the blueprint. About breaking cycles not just for herself but for everyone watching to see that it is possible.

She started small. She picked up a few things about stocks and the stock market. Nothing glamorous. Around this time, she focused on the safe long-term investments that would build over time, that would increase earned revenue in ways a salary alone never would.

The fall after getting her associate's degree, she transferred to UT Arlington. She had registered for more classes, still had work... but the science of balancing everything was still something she was figuring out.

After completing her first year there she had gone to speak with an academic advisor to get a better understanding of where she stood in her degree plan. That advisor had her under the impression that she had one more year left. One year. She had been holding onto that number like a baby holds on to someone's finger, like hope that the finish line was visible even if still distant.

The following semester she went back to speak with another advisor for a check in. This time she was paired with a senior advisor who had reviewed her transcripts and had done the updated calculations for her.

Cadence hung on the silence, hoping for good news, but the atmosphere grew leaden. The air in the room seemed to thicken with a sudden, heavy dread. The hope in her eyes vanished as they looked at each other and it was replaced by the look of someone who already knew the news wasn't good... and she knew it before a single word was spoken.

"You have two more years left," the senior advisor said. "Not one. Two."

Cadence sat there. Processed the words. Two years. Two more years. Not one. Two.

She fought back tears as she walked out of the building. Held them in through the hallway, through the campus, all the way to her car. She got in. Closed the door. Then the container she had been holding everything in shattered.

She started hyperventilating. Couldn't catch her breath. Couldn't think past the number two, past the realization that she had been wrong about her own timeline, that it was going to take even longer than the long it had already taken. She screamed. Banged on the steering wheel with fists that wanted to hit something sturdier, something that could absorb the rage, frustration and exhaustion that had nowhere else to go.

Then the tears came. Not the gentle type. She didn't quiet cry. The tears gushed out like water from a fireman's hose, violent, and unstoppable, and releasing everything she had been holding back for years. The disappointment. The fear. The feeling of being trapped in a system that kept moving the finish line every time she had gotten close.

She called Brandon. Tried to explain through the scream-crying and hyperventilating. She wasn't sure he could understand her through the sounds that weren't quite words, through the breakdown that felt too big for her body to contain.

He understood enough, though. He gave her space to let it all out. Didn't try to fix it immediately. Didn't tell her to calm down or that it was not that bad. He just let her feel it, all of it, until the wave crested and started to recede.

When she could breathe again, he spoke.

"It's okay," he said. His voice calm, steady, and with the kind of certainty she needed when her own had collapsed. "It's just time. I know that despite the misfortune, you're going to get through it. You're going to make it across the finish line."

She sat there in her car, tears still on her face, breathing still uneven. Heard what he was really saying: You are not failing. You are just taking longer than you expected. Longer doesn't mean never. You still have time.

She made it home. Sat with what had happened. Something inside of her altered in a way that changed her mindset on how she needed to start approaching life.

She got intentional. Really intentional. About not giving up. About breaking the cycle. About being the one in the family who puts footprints in the sand for the generations that would come after her. This was not just about getting a degree anymore. This was about proving that it was possible. That someone from her family, with her background and with her specific set of obstacles, could still make things happen.

That moment in her car changed her. Made her even more resilient than before. This was when she started maturing – not just getting older but growing up in the ways that are internal but projected externally. Cadence was understanding that struggle doesn't disqualify you from success. That even if it takes seven years to get a four-year degree it doesn't mean you are less than people who did it in four. It just means your path was longer. Longer paths build different muscles.

Things got harder in ways Cadence had not expected. She started gaining weight. Not a lot at first, but enough to notice. Enough to feel it. She was getting depressed – not dramatically to where anyone else could see, but in that low-grade way that makes everything feel heavier than it should. She hid it pretty well. Kept pushing along. Because she had to keep going. Like Dory in Finding Nemo, she had to just keep swimming. Just keep swimming. Even when you are tired. Even when you cannot see through the water. Just keep swimming.

She still was not socializing the way Brandon wanted her to. She still drove to campus, went to class, and went straight home. Being social took energy she was using just to survive. Friendships felt like amenities she couldn't afford when she was trying to balance school and work and the weight of knowing she was taking longer than everyone expected.

Music had become something else by now. Somewhere after getting her associate's degree, she had let go of the record deal dream completely. She had no choice but to let it go as opposed to just pushing it aside for later. She realized that her music could just be a hobby. That she was no longer in her prime – or at least, no longer in the narrow window the music industry cared about. But, that didn't matter, because she knew that music would never have an ending in her life. It would live on with her as long as she did. So, she still made music. She still sang. She even kept some updated tracks on her website. Despite it still being her escape, it was not the escape route that she had previously envisioned anymore. It was just part of who she was. Part of her identity that no longer needed to save her to matter.

She could never let music go entirely. It was woven too deeply into how she understood herself. It didn't have to be everything, though. It could just be something she loved without needing it to love her back in specific, tangible, measurable ways.

Two more years. That was the sentence she served after the breakdown. Two years of grueling classes and double shifts; of balancing on a wire and crying in the quiet; of pushing through, watching the scale tip back and forth, masking the hollow ache of depression, and just... keeping her head above water.

She just kept swimming.

Chapter 12

Seven Years, One Crossing

✦ — ✦

Seven years total – that was the price of what it had cost her. It was a seven-year journey to reach a four-year destination, a timeline stretched thin by the sheer weight of everything she had been forced to carry.

By the time graduation finally arrived in the spring of 2020, Cadence was twenty-five years old. She was years behind the schedule she had once scribbled into the margins of her notebooks, and miles past the point of simple exhaustion.

The version of herself that eventually crossed the stage was older, more frayed, and far more substantial than the girl who had started. She held the degree in her hand, the paper crisp and absolute, but she knew she had traded more of her youth for it than she had ever intended. It had left her with a weariness that went bone-deep, the kind sleep couldn't touch.

She had finished, though. Against the odds, against the breakdowns, and against the voices that suggested she might just be a girl who *started things but didn't finish*, Cadence had done it.

The world had tilted on its axis by then. The pandemic arrived like a sudden winter, turning the concept of "normal" into a relic of a bygone era. Streets fell silent and the future felt fragile, but Cadence found herself unexpectedly prepared. Her earlier pivot to IT meant that being locked away didn't mean being left behind. She had discovered the ultimate hedge against uncertainty – a profession that didn't just survive the plague, but thrived in its digital shadow. It was stable. It was lucrative. And at long last, it was a foundation.

If it took her seven years to do what others did in four, it only meant she had carried more weight on the climb. She realized now that every sacrifice had been a calculated move, and every time she pulled over to cry in her car was merely a pit stop, not a finish line.

She arrived at that graduation ceremony with a dignity forged in fire, not given as a gift. She didn't just walk across the stage – she claimed it. Her stride carried a victory that those on shorter, smoother paths could never fully grasp, because she had paid for her seat with a currency of persistence the four-year students didn't even know existed.

The transition into the workforce, however, proved to be its own cruel gauntlet. After earning her degree, she needed a way to sustain the mounting responsibilities of her life, but the market felt like a locked door. She submitted application after application, only to receive rejection letters in return. She found herself trapped in the suffocating irony of the entry-level seeker: every "junior" role demanded years of experience she didn't have, yet no one was willing to be the one to give her that experience.

She received so many no's that rejection became background ambiance – a steady hum of discouragement. In a moment of defiant desperation, she began applying for roles she felt wildly unqualified for, positions at the highest levels, just to see if anyone would even bat an eye or offer a phone interview.

The company she eventually landed at was a well-known IT titan, a global giant that received millions of applications for a mere handful of roles. It was the kind of place that usually filtered out anyone without a perfect, linear pedigree. Yet they were the ones who finally looked closer.

During the interview, Cadence didn't hide the life she had lived. She let them see the crookedness in her smile – a physical testament to grit and years of *just keep swimming*. She told her story not as a list of grievances, but as evidence of resilience.

They didn't just see a résumé; they saw the strength beneath it. They recognized that while she lacked the polished experience of a traditional hire, she possessed a tenacity that couldn't be taught in any boardroom. They saw her potential – and they took a chance on her.

Suddenly, the *money consciousness* seed Brandon had planted all those years ago began to bloom into something tangible. With a salary that finally matched her worth, Cadence started doing more with her investments, moving beyond the paycheck and into stocks, crypto, and other assets. As those investments began to pay off, the lesson crystallized: money first, security first – then everything else gets to exist without the frantic heartbeat of desperation.

She was different now. More reserved than the confident, bubbly girl she'd been in middle school, but far more secure. She was certain about what mattered. Less concerned with being liked. More committed to being respected. Less interested in quick wins, and fully devoted to the long game.

She wanted to be the blueprint.

She was already leaving her footprints in the sand, becoming living proof that it was possible to survive the wreckage and build something grander on top of it. As she looked back at the shadow of the eight-year-old she once was, a quiet understanding passed between them.

That child – small, scared, but fiercely determined – had made a vow in the darkness of a world that felt too big and too cold. A sacred promise to find a way out. To bridge the gap between survival and success. To make something of herself.

She carried that oath for seventeen years – not just for her own sake, but for her mother, and for every person who would one day be told that their circumstances were their destiny, that they simply weren't enough.

Standing there at twenty-five, degree in hand and a future finally secured, Cadence sent a whisper back through time to the child still waiting in the dark. She let her know she had delivered on every word of the promise.

The path had been longer. The smile more worn. The heart far more tired.

But she had kept her word.

REFLECTION FOUR

Thirty years later, the horizon is clear,

The rhythm is steady, the music is here.

Not built for the stadium, or lights, or the crowd,

But a whisper that hums through the ribs, deep and proud.

Her locs are a crown she has chosen to wear,

A legacy woven through intention and prayer.

She no longer bends till she's certain to snap,

She has folded the blueprint and burnt every map.

The first note was breathing, the last note is free,

The song is her own—as she was meant to be.

PART FIVE

LEARNING THE TEMPO

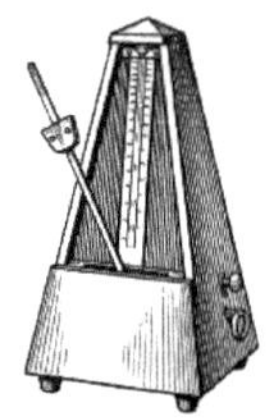

Chapter 13

Building the Base

✦—✦

The transition into 2021 arrived with a jarring dissonance. Cadence was now armed with a degree, standing in the middle of a global pandemic, and stranded in the kind of pervasive uncertainty that forces a person to either freeze in place or adapt at lightning speed.

Cadence, however, was already a professional at this kind of pivot. If she thought about it, she had been practicing the art of adaptation her entire life – weathering storms through sheer resilience. What was one more gust of wind to a woman who had already survived so many?

The world was still reeling, caught in a strange liminal space of face masks, panic-buying toilet paper, and social distancing. But for Cadence, the year marked the first true anchor in her professional life.

She landed her first career-track job as an Associate Developer. It was entry-level IT, but the title felt like a royal decree. It served as validation that the seven-year odyssey had been worth every tear cried in the front seat of her car – and everywhere else, for that matter. For the first time, she was doing work that required that specific piece of paper, work that demanded the precise set of skills she had labored to earn.

The company provided training, a blessing she welcomed with open arms. She quickly learned that academic theory and professional practice were often different languages that merely shared vocabulary. The classroom had given her the words; the job was teaching her how to speak.

Because the world was still operating under the shadow of COVID, her introduction to the industry was entirely remote. This became her oasis. Behind a muted microphone and a turned-off webcam, she could learn from the quiet of her own home. She could make mistakes without an audience, build competence in stillness, and hide the heat of embarrassment whenever she stumbled over a line of code or forgot a semicolon.

In a world that felt fundamentally unstable, IT became her citadel. It meant an income that didn't depend on physical presence in a crowded office. It meant a career path resilient enough to survive global disruption. At long last, it was a future she could touch.

By 2022, the stability of her career began to show in her personal evolution. She decided to start her locs – a choice that felt deeply symbolic, even if she struggled to articulate why. It was a step toward self-acceptance, a commitment to a natural process that couldn't be rushed, a transformation allowed to unfold on its own timeline.

Beneath the aesthetic, however, was a harder logic.

She hadn't done as much research as she probably should have before sitting in the chair; she simply knew she wanted them, and she was done postponing her own desires. Starting her locs ensured that her presence in corporate America would exist on her own terms. It became a visible marker of becoming. In environments that historically struggled to accept people who looked like her, wearing her hair in locs felt like a quiet but firm stance.

It wasn't theatrical protest. It was belonging without permission.

That same year, she took her next baby step – a better position at the same company, with a slightly higher salary. She wasn't scrambling up ladders in a frenzy. She was ascending with slow, intentional grace.

Each step was deliberate. Each move calculated. Brandon had taught her long ago that most wealth wasn't built through dramatic leaps, but through consistent, strategic decisions that compounded over time. She was finally seeing the math of those lessons play out in her own life.

But Cadence soon learned a universal truth: there is a specific intoxication that comes with having money after a lifetime of not having enough.

With a steady income flowing in, the fear of the well drying up began to fade. In its place grew a subtle frivolity.

She started spending like someone who had forgotten the taste of hunger. The survival tools that once guided her – budgeting, restraint, foresight – slowly drifted into the background. She was enjoying the fruit of her labor, but losing sight of the orchard.

Brandon noticed first. He didn't need to see her bank statements. He saw it in the packages arriving at her door, the shift in how she talked about weekends, the quiet disappearance of the word *budget* from her vocabulary.

The conversation didn't happen in a boardroom or over spreadsheets. It happened with the casual honesty that had defined their friendship since high school. When the moment felt still enough, he leveled with her.

"You're playing a dangerous game, Cadence," he said, his voice stripped of humor. "I've watched you climb for years to get to this view. Don't get so dizzy looking at the top that you forget how to stay there."

He reminded her that her salary was a tool, not the destination. He named lifestyle creep – the silent predator that eats away at success until you're left with nicer things and the same old desperation. He urged her to see unnecessary spending not as rewards, but as leaks in a ship she had spent nearly a decade building.

"The goal wasn't just to have money," Brandon said. "It was to build a foundation that can't be shaken. Right now, you're choosing the thrill of the buy over the peace of the base."

The words stung because they were true. Cadence felt the familiar heat of embarrassment – the same heat she once hid behind turned-off webcams. She realized she had grown careless with the very thing meant to free her. She had treated income like a battery to be drained instead of a seed to be planted.

But course correction had always been her strength.

She didn't get defensive. She got disciplined.

She thanked Brandon, stripped back the excess, reopened her spreadsheets, and realigned herself with the long game. She returned to the track she had spent seven years fighting to find.

The reward came at twenty-six, when she reached her first major financial milestone. Cadence bought her first car.

It was hers. Purchased with her money. Her credit. Her signature alone on the title. It wasn't just transportation – it was independence made tangible.

Yet she knew success wasn't only about acquisition. It was also about what you were stable enough to give away.

Remembering her own early desperation, she passed her old car down to her younger cousin for her sixteenth birthday. It was a gift of freedom. A widening of possibility. Her way of ensuring that the cycle of *being enough* reached someone she loved.

By the end of 2022, the wealth-building mindset that began as a seed had become a forest. Brandon's lessons had finally sunk roots deep enough to sustain them. She moved beyond dabbling and into intention, no longer saving just for emergencies, but constructing infrastructure for the future.

She began to understand how money moved. She stopped thinking in terms of *enough* and started thinking in terms of *choice*. She was building a foundation sturdy enough to allow decisions guided by desire, not debt.

Looking back over the first twenty-six years of her life, the pieces finally assembled into something whole. She wasn't just a girl who had worked hard.

She was a woman who had built a path forward.

Chapter 14

The Architecture

✦ — ✦

Cadence finally understood the weight of the *money consciousness* seed Brandon had planted all those years ago. What began as a quiet realization had matured into disciplined practice. She moved beyond simply watching the market and into making deliberate moves – stocks, crypto, and eventually the solid ground of real estate.

These were investments designed to compound over time, to build wealth in ways a salary alone never could.

The lesson had finally clicked.

Money first.
Security first.
Only when the foundation is ironclad does the rest of life get to exist

without the frantic heartbeat of desperation.

The girl she once was had been replaced by someone almost unrecognizable. She was quieter now, but more substantial, moving with the kind of certainty that only comes from surviving the climb. The desire to be liked had fallen away, revealed as a poor substitute for being respected. The girl who chased quick wins had given way to a woman committed to the long game.

In the spring of 2023, at twenty-eight years old, Cadence bought her first piece of real estate.

It wasn't a condo.
It wasn't a starter unit.

It was an entire house.

A property that was hers – to rent, to leverage, to grow. An asset that could generate income while appreciating in value. In every traditional sense, she had achieved the American Dream: degree, job, car, house.

But Cadence knew better.

Brandon had taught her that the American Dream was often just a parable – one designed to convince the extraordinary to be content inside a box they were never meant to inhabit. It was a formula for staying in the rat race. Real wealth came from having the audacity to question what you had been taught to want.

She refused to trade freedom for accumulation. She had watched too many people exchange autonomy for objects that eventually owned them. Instead, she viewed capital as a tool – a lever capable of prying open a future that belonged to her. She wasn't interested in the appearance of wealth.

She was obsessed with the mechanics of it.

By the fall of 2024, that discipline bore its most significant fruit yet. She pushed beyond the safety of her first property and purchased a second home. This wasn't an emotional decision or a bid for status. It was cold. Calculated. Strategic.

Another asset.
Another layer.
Another stepping stone.

Each deed felt like armor – protection forged to ensure the apprehension of her youth remained a ghost rather than a threat.

Brandon hadn't just given her a map; he had invited her onto the field. Their relationship evolved from advice into partnership as they co-founded ventures that forced Cadence to test her instincts in real time. She became a co-owner of a martial arts student management portal, an e-commerce platform, and a real estate investment group.

This was her venture-capital education.

A masterclass taught not through textbooks, but through the daily responsibility of keeping something alive. She learned quickly that there was no better way to understand the heartbeat of a business than to be accountable for its survival.

Their partnership took physical form when they tackled a fix-and-flip project together. The property they started with was barely a house – more slab than shelter. It had to be stripped down to the studs before it could be reborn.

The process was grueling. Dusty. Unforgiving.

Cadence thrived in it.

When the renovation was complete, the transformation was so precise that other investors began using the house as a blueprint for their own projects.

For Cadence, it was more than a profit margin.

It was proof.

Proof that her mind was capable of more than executing instructions for someone else's vision.

Standing in the finished space, she realized she had discovered a different kind of artistry. She could create more than a song. She could build more than an album. She could transform vision into structure – ideas into income. The creativity she once reserved for music had expanded into something larger: legacy.

But the architecture of her life wasn't only changing on balance sheets and property deeds.

Her relationship with her mother – once tense and riddled with unspoken things – began a quiet evolution. They moved beyond obligatory check-ins and hollow *how are yous*, carving out space for intentional connection. They aligned schedules not out of duty, but desire.

With time, the sharp edges of their history softened. They learned the difficult art of communication – shifting from talking at one another to actually listening. Distance had been a harsh teacher, but it provided the perspective neither had possessed while trapped in the same orbit. Time became a benefactor, offering grace enough to prioritize the present over the past.

This same evolution extended to her siblings. Relationships once strained by proximity and upheaval settled into something functional – sometimes even sturdy. Cadence, ever the strategist, began to view these dynamics differently. She realized that the people who knew her best were often the most challenging to navigate.

And so she practiced.

She treated family interactions as a training ground, refining the same skills she was developing professionally – leadership, empathy, boundary-setting. It was messy. Imperfect. But deeply instructive. By navigating her own bloodline, she gained an education in human behavior more visceral than anything a textbook could offer.

She learned that to build a world, one must first learn how to maintain the people within it.

Along the way, she also made a crucial distinction: relatives were bound by blood or paperwork; family was built through reciprocity. Cadence had grown tired of one-sided relationships of any kind – of always being the one to reach out, accommodate, bend.

She wanted balance.

She demanded it – not loudly, but decisively. Through the quiet refusal to accept less. If a relationship didn't move in both directions, it was no longer one she was willing to maintain.

That clarity became her freedom.

Music found its way back to her, though in a gentler form. It no longer carried the weight of escape or survival. It simply existed as part of her – a quiet, essential room in the house she had built of herself.

The girl who once dreamed of stadium lights and record deals had been laid to rest. In her place stood a different kind of artist. Cadence began creating again, not in pursuit of validation, but because melodies once more crowded her mind and demanded somewhere to live.

The *triple threat* Brandon had once envisioned – singer, writer, producer – had finally materialized, but entirely on her terms. She wasn't building for an industry that might discard her. She was building for a small, trusted audience. More importantly, she was building for herself.

There was a quiet power in realizing the music hadn't saved her.

She had done the work of saving herself, with help, grit, and discipline. The music was no longer her life raft.

It was the scenery.

Looking at the life she had assembled – the degrees, the career, the assets, the hard-won peace – she knew she had accomplished what she set out to do. She had broken the cycle she was born into, not through spectacle or applause, but through steady, relentless persistence.

And that had always been her way.

Chapter 15

A Tempo of Her Own

✦—✦

By the time Cadence turned thirty; the horizon of her life had shifted. For the first time, her decisions were purely her own – untethered from the need to prove a point or fulfill expectations planted by others. She was no longer performing for an audience.

She was finally living for herself.

This clarity revealed itself in the smallest, most personal choices. She decided to restart her loc journey, setting aside the rushed, ambiguous set she had begun in her twenties. She wanted locs that felt intentional, versatile, reflective of her actual taste. What seemed like a minor reset carried significant weight – it was a declaration that she was no longer in a hurry to be finished, and no longer willing to settle for *good enough*.

She began prioritizing her own happiness with a ferocity she had once denied herself. She learned the art of checking in with herself first, ensuring her foundation was steady before reaching out to support anyone else. The days of setting herself on fire to keep others warm were over.

Her strength now wasn't just visible – it was internal.

She hadn't become this woman *in spite* of struggle, but because of it. The extended timelines. The breakdowns. The quiet battles with depression. The music dreams she once buried. All of it had been raw material, used to build someone solid – someone who knew her worth because she had fought to establish it.

Cadence hadn't merely talked about breaking the cycle. She dismantled it – brick by brick.

She became the first in her family to earn a four-year degree. She moved beyond earning a paycheck and into building wealth with intention, understanding that success wasn't found in consumption, but in ownership – what you built to work for you.

She became the blueprint.

Her life formed a set of footprints in the sand, proof for the generations coming after her that someone from their background, with their obstacles, could finish what they started. Because of her, her nieces and nephews would grow up knowing college was an option, not a fantasy. They would understand that struggle was a season, not a sentence – because they had watched her escape.

She had the receipts.

At thirty, Cadence finally understood what had eluded her at seventeen: bending was not the same as breaking. Bending was flexibility – the quiet strength of a willow in a storm, touching the ground without losing the power to rise again.

She had bent beneath grief. Beneath expectation. Beneath the weight of being *the first*. There were nights she was certain she would snap clean in two.

But she didn't break.

She bent – and in that bending, she learned what breaking never could have taught her.

She looked nothing like what she had survived. When she met her reflection now, she didn't flinch or search for flaws. She saw someone she recognized. Someone she trusted.

Cadence – a name defined by rhythm, by the pattern that keeps a song moving even when the melody falters – had finally found her tempo. It wasn't the overzealous beat she imagined in her teens or the desperate rhythm of her twenties. It was a pace uniquely her own, waiting for her to become still enough to hear it.

The song wasn't over. It would never truly be over.

But it had found its progression.

Survival had been the goal for so long that she had nearly forgotten there was a world beyond it. When survival stopped being the mission, she learned how to live.

And living – without apology, permission, or fear of the fall – turned out to be the greatest rebellion of all.

Turning thirty wasn't an ending.

It was an awakening.

She was strong.
She was whole.

And she was just getting started.

EPILOGUE
THE MEASURE OF THE SONG

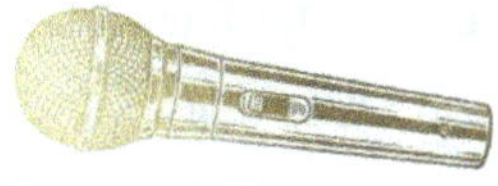

Some people are born with names that arrive empty – names without meaning, meant to be filled by force, by accident, by ambition, or by regret. They spend their lives trying to give their names weight, manufacturing significance where none was promised.

Cadence was not one of them.

She was named for movement.
For rhythm.
For the rise and fall that governs all frequencies – though she didn't know this at first.

For a long time, she only knew the sound of her name, not the ancient wisdom hidden inside its syllables.

When she was young, the rhythm felt punishing. Every beat landed too hard or too fast – a jagged percussion that left her breathless and bruised. Life moved out of tempo: relocations before roots could form, loss before language could catch up, silence where answers should have lived.

She believed something was wrong with her. That everyone else had been given a roadmap she somehow missed.

In those scrambling years, she mistook disruption for failure. She mistook the weight of her life for a solo instead of a complete song. Most of all, she mistook bending for breaking.

What she couldn't yet see was that she was carrying more than her own weight. She carried the ancestral echo of Black women who had forgotten how to exhale – women whose rhythms were dictated by the seasons of others, whose lives moved to the frantic beat of *not enough.*

Their music was endurance.
A hymn of making do.

Cadence heard those ghosts in her blood, and her greatest fear was becoming another verse in that ancient song.

That fear shaped the anatomy of her bend.

It was internal. Invisible. A stretching few ever saw. She bent beneath instability that never allowed roots to form. Beneath inherited responsibility that taught her to shrink. Beneath grief that arrived before it could be named.

The world demanded elasticity long before it offered safety.

She learned to bend not because she was fragile, but because rigid things break.

This kind of bending is labor. It requires carrying weight so precisely that no one else feels the tilt. To avoid becoming a burden, she mastered the art of quiet resurrection – falling apart in the dark and rebuilding herself before daylight could catch her in pieces.

She believed that if she reached a certain number, a certain title, a certain version of *fine*, she would finally be allowed to stand straight.

What she knows now is this: her song had been moving through her all along – in how she endured, how she listened, how she adapted instead of disappearing.

Now she looks in the mirror and sees someone familiar. Someone shaped by pressure, not defined by it. Someone who carries her past without being crushed beneath it.

Healing didn't erase the scars.

It taught her how to move beautifully around them.

She looks at her locs – a crown chosen with intention – and sees a woman who blossomed not despite the struggle, but because of it.

She has reached the rare independence of *not needing*.

Not needing permission.
Not needing approval.
Not needing to filter every heartbeat through survival.

What she craves now is choice.

The ability to say *yes* because her soul is full.
The ability to say *no* without guilt reaching for her sleeve.

She has a plan – one that sways her to sleep like a rocking chair. If the numbers hold, she will reach financial independence before forty.

What comes after remains unwritten.

And for the first time, the blank page is not terror.

It is invitation.

She was never meant to outrun the rhythm.

She was meant to learn it.
To move with it.
To trust it – even when the melody fell away.

Cadence, who once chased songs she couldn't hold, finally recognizes this one – not because it is perfect, but because it is true.

The first note was a breath.
The last note will be a legacy.

And at long last, the song is hers.

From the Author:

Thank you for reading this story. If it resonated with you, I'd love to stay connected!

I build community through Mellow Mastermind — a space for those who are done just surviving and are ready to design the life that they deserve.

Find me at:

- www.officiallymars.com

- @MellowMastermind on Instagram, YouTube, and TikTok

- Mellow Mastermind Community Server on Discord

- LinkTr.ee/ WandaMars

I'm also available for speaking engagements, workshops, and corporate creativity training. Let's connect!

www.ingramcontent.com/pod-product-compliance
Lightning Source LLC
LaVergne TN
LVHW010903110826
845149LV00005B/1451